FEVER

How Tu Youyou Adapted Traditional Chinese Medicine to Find a Cure for Malaria

Moments in Science

by Darcy Pattison
Illustrated by Peter Willis

FEVER: How Tu Youyou used Traditional Chinese Medicine to Find a Cure for Malaria
Written by Darcy Pattison
Illustrated by Peter Willis

Mims House
1309 Broadway
Little Rock, AR 72202
MimsHouseBooks.com

Publisher's Cataloging-in-Publication data

Names: Pattison, Darcy, author. | Peter Willis, illustrator.
Title: Fever : how Tu Youyou used traditional Chinese medicine to find a cure for malaria / by Darcy Pattison; illustrated by Peter Willis.
Series: Moments in Science.
Description: Little Rock, AR: Little Rock, AR, 2022. | Summary: Follow the struggles of Nobel Prize scientist Tu Youyou as she works to find a medicine for malaria.
Identifiers: LCCN: 2021921328 | ISBN: 9781629441955 (hardcover) | 9781629441962 (paperback) | 9781629441979 (ebook) | 9781629441986 (audio)
Subjects: LCSH Tu, Youyou, 1930---Juvenile literature. | Pharmacologists--China--Biography--Juvenile literature. | Medical scientists--China--Biography--Juvenile literature. | Women in science--Biography--Juvenile literature. | Malaria--Treatment--Juvenile literature. | Medicine, Chinese--Juvenile literature. | BISAC JUVENILE NONFICTION / Science & Nature / History of Science | JUVENILE NONFICTION / Health & Daily Living / Diseases, Illnesses & Injuries | JUVENILE NONFICTION / Biography & Autobiography / Science & Technology | JUVENILE NONFICTION / Biography & Autobiography / Women | JUVENILE NONFICTION / People & Places / Asia
Classification: LCC RS73.T83 P38 2022 | DDC 615.1/092--dc23

Thanks to Zheng-Yu Li, May Waye, Ph.D, of the Chinese University of Hong Kong, and Chiu Kin, Ph.D. of the University of Hong Kong for checking the accuracy of the text.

Photo Permission: Woodcut portrait of Ge Hong https://wellcomecollection.org/works/f65bzfbc/items,

RESOURCES
The World Health Organization maintains statistics and data on malaria outbreaks in the world: https://www.who.int/news-room/fact-sheets/detail/malaria

Liu Liping, Tu Youyou: China's First Female Nobel Prize Winner, London: ACA Publishing Ltd., in association with the People's Publishing House, Beijing, China: 2016

The Nobel Prize organization's information about Tu Youyou (accessed November 19, 2021):
Acceptance speech: https://www.nobelprize.org/prizes/medicine/2015/tu/lecture/
Biography: https://www.nobelprize.org/prizes/medicine/2015/tu/biographical/
Hear Tu Youyou's voice in this Interview: https://www.nobelprize.org/prizes/medicine/2015/tu/interview/

The problem was clear:

people were dying of malaria, called *nüèjí* (NEW-e-jee) in Chinese. It is a deadly disease that causes a fever that comes and goes, chills, and often death.

Tu Youyou, a 39-year-old medical researcher, opened a traditional Chinese medicine book that was almost 1,630 years old.

Writing in 340 A.D., Ge Hong said, "To reduce fever, take a handful of sweet wormwood, soak it in about 'er sheng,' [about two liters of water], squeeze out the juice, and drink it all."

Youyou added sweet wormwood (*Artemisia annua*) to the list of plants to test as a malaria medicine.

It was 1969, and Youyou was part of a People's Republic of China task force called Project 523 that was searching for a new anti-malaria medicine. The stakes were high: worldwide, the yearly death count from malaria was over half a million people.

Malaria is caused by

Plasmodium parasites.

A parasite is an organism that lives on or in another organism called the host. The parasite gets its food from the host organism.

The *Plasmodium* parasite lives inside *Anopheles* mosquitoes. When a mosquito bites a human, the parasite can enter the human body. Then the human becomes the host for the parasite.

The *Plasmodium* parasite that caused malaria was becoming drug-resistant to many of the old medicines. Drug resistance happens when a microorganism has changed and a drug doesn't kill it any longer.

Doctors needed a new, fast-acting, and long-lasting drug.

People were dying!

Working alone at first.

Youyou researched old medical books. In April 1969, she sent *A Collection of Secret Proven Prescriptions for Malaria*, a report that contained 640 recipes for traditional Chinese medicines for malaria.

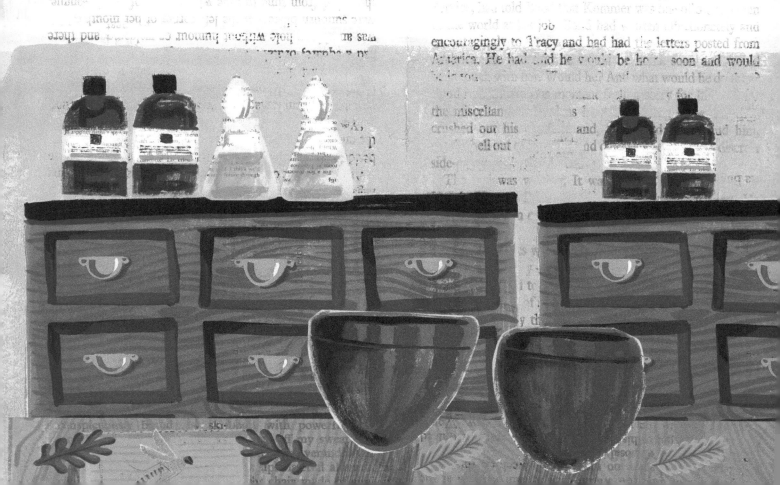

Youyou knew how to force compounds out of plants, a process called extraction.

Laboratory equipment was scarce, so Youyou used large clay pots. Sometimes, she boiled the plants in water, and sometimes she soaked them in chemicals. Then, like squeezing water out of a sponge, she squeezed out the compounds to test. Within a month, she had 50 compounds, or extracts, ready to test against the malaria parasite in mice.

At first, exciting news came back! An extract from a pepper plant weakened the malaria parasite in 85% of infected mice.

But more research showed that it didn't kill the parasite.

In the summer of 1969,

Youyou joined other researchers on Hainan Island to test extracts on sick people, instead of just mice.

In the Hainan rainforests, Youyou saw for the first time how malaria affects the human body. The researchers tried extracts from peppers and chilies. But nothing worked.

For two years, Youyou tried to find a plant extract that would work, but everything failed.

BY 1971,

Youyou and her three assistants had tested more than 200 compounds taken from over 100 traditional Chinese medicine recipes. Looking over all the data, they saw that the best extract was only 40% effective.

Stubborn, Youyou said, "Let's immerse ourselves in reading the medical books again!"

She had read the anicent books so often that the edges of the pages were starting to curl.

One Plant interested Youyou.

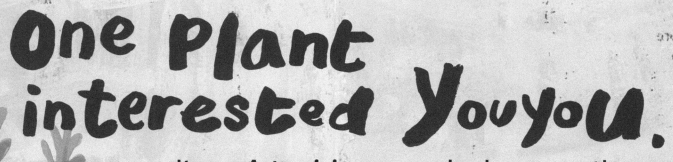

It was *Artemisia* annua, also known as the herb qinghao (JING-how). It was a pungent plant often used in perfumes or to flavor foods and drinks. But the *Artemisia* extracts didn't work against malaria.

One day, Youyou read Ge Hong's book again. It said to soak the plant in water and then squeeze out the juice. But Youyou had been boiling the plants to extract compounds. Youyou wondered if the heat might change the compounds. She also wondered if there were different compounds in the leaves and plant stems.

In September 1971, Youyou designed a new way of extracting the compounds at lower temperatures and using different parts of the plant. Using the new technique, the team began the long process of retesting every plant they had tested before.

Again, they had 190 failures.

But on October 4, 1971.

the test results came back for the extract number 191. The *Artemisia annua* extract had killed 100% of the malaria parasite in mice and in monkeys.

   The researchers worried about toxic side-effects. Three of the researchers, including Youyou, tested the extract on themselves. When it was successful, they tested it on patients in Beijing and on Hainan Island.

Everyone got well.

The world had a new cure for malaria.

For discovering a new medicine for malaria, Youyou was awarded the 2015 Nobel Prize in Physiology or Medicine. It was the fourth time the Nobel Prize had been awarded for research on malaria, and the first time the Nobel was awarded to a Chinese woman.

When she accepted the Nobel Prize, youyou said,

"Artemisinin... is a true gift from old Chinese medicine. ... Every scientist dreams of doing something that can help the world."

Tu Youyou

Chinese chemist and medical researcher Tu Youyou was born in the port city of Zhejiang Ningbo on December 20, 1930. She became ill with tuberculosis at age 16, which inspired her to study medicine. At Beijing Medical College, she learned to apply western medical science to the traditional Chinese medicines. Her first research project used a traditional herb, *Lobelia chinensis*, to treat snail fever, or Schistosomiasis, a disease of the intestines and urinary tract that is caused by parasitic flatworms.

Youyou was the lead researcher for a military research project called Project 523, so named because it was created at a meeting on May 23. During the Vietnam War, soldiers were four to five times more likely to die from malaria than from fighting. North Vietnam asked China for help in discovering a new medicine. Youyou's job was to search for a cure for malaria, by testing prescriptions from old Chinese medical texts. From 1969 to 1972, over 240,000 compounds were tested but they all failed.

The research was accomplished at great personal sacrifices. Youyou's two daughters were mostly raised by family or friends. At one point, she didn't see her young daughters for three years. Youyou developed health problems from the research chemicals, and one fellow researcher, Cui Shulian, died from the toxic chemicals. Youyou also volunteered to test the medicine for side effects by taking it herself. In spite of all the problems, Youyou persevered and developed artemisinin to treat malaria. In 2015, she became the first Chinese woman to receive the Nobel Prize in Physiology or Medicine for her malaria drug.

The Malaria Parasite-*Plasmodium falciparum*

With a complicated life cycle, the *Plasmodium falciparum* parasite lives part of its life inside a mosquito's gut and part inside a human's liver and blood cells. When in a human, the parasite multiplies rapidly and causes the illness we call malaria. The disease, among other symptoms, causes fever and shaking chills that starts about 10 to 15 days after being bit by a female mosquito. In 2018, the World Health Organization (https://www.who.int/news-room/fact-sheets/detail/malaria) reported that over half the world's population is at risk for malaria, with the highest risk in Africa. Malaria kills over 400,000 people each year. About two-thirds of fatalities are children under the age of five.

ANOPHELES MOSQUITO

Known as the dapple-winged mosquito, the female Anopheles mosquito can give malaria to people. The mosquito is secretive and nocturnal, feeding at night when people are asleep. They usually feed on plant nectar. However, to lay eggs, the female needs a meal of blood. One way to prevent malaria is to kill mosquitoes. Scientists study the mosquito life cycle and try to stop it at each stage. Because it usually bites between dusk and dawn, one prevention method is to put insecticide mosquito netting around a bed. Spraying insecticides inside a house is another method. Often cities will try to prevent standing water, which is needed for the mosquito life cycle.

HISTORY OF MALARIA RESEARCH

1820 French chemists Pierre Joseph Pelletier (1788-1842) and Jean Bienamé Caventou (1795-1877) extracted quinine, a malaria medicine, from the bitter bark of the South American cinchona tree.

1902 The Nobel Prize is awarded to British doctor Ronald Ross (1857-1932) of the British Indian Medical Service for discovering the mosquito stages of malaria.

1907 The Nobel Prize is awarded to French army doctor Charles Louis Alphonse Laveran (1845-1922) for discovering the *Plasmodium* parasite that causes malaria.

1934 Chloroquine, a synthetic substitute for quinine, is developed by German chemical company I.G. Farben.

1948 Swiss scientist Paul Müller (1899-1965) is awarded the Nobel Prize for discovering DDT, an insecticide that kills mosquitoes and was used to control malaria and yellow fever. Today, DDT is banned because of its environmental effects.

1971 Artemisinin is derived from the *Artemisia annua* (sweet wormwood) plant, by the Project 523, led by Tu Youyou.

1974 Mefloquine is developed by the U.S. Army Medical Research and Developmental Command, the World Health Organization, and Hoffman-La-Roche, Inc.

2015 Tu Youyou awarded the Nobel Prize in Physiology or Medicine for her discovery of artemisinin to treat malaria.

2021 The World Health Organization recommends the malaria vaccine Mosquirix for protecting young children. Previous drugs treated malaria after a person became sick. But the vaccine will prevent people from getting the malaria disease. It's hailed as a breakthrough that can save many lives.

MOMENTS IN SCIENCE

Scan the QR Code for more about Moments in Science books.

Printed in the USA
CPSIA information can be obtained
at www.ICGtesting.com
LVHW060745100124
768537LV00003BA/25